All rights reserved. No part of this book may be reproduced or transmitted in any way, electronically or mechanically. No photocopying or any information storage system, without permission from the publisher. This is a work of fiction, a product of the author's imagination.

Library of Congress #2021921418
ISBN #978-17378682-1-7
ISBN #978-1-7378682-2-4

Dedication

To my Dad, Otis Seward. He grew the best tasting vegetables in Virginia.

To a little puppy like Seward the garden behind the house is big. Almost like a farm in the country!

Like all puppies, Seward likes to wake up early each morning. He hears the geese honk and runs over to play.

He is surprised to see a beautiful butterfly fly next to his head. Seward walks slowly over to see it.

Seward follows the farmer between the rows of tall bean plants. Seward likes to eat green beans.

Seward sees the shovel and rake. They help the farmer plant the vegetable seeds.

He wiggles under the fence and hides in the grass.

Did another puppy hide purple balls in a hole?
No, these are beets for the family to eat.

Seward thinks the red balls on the plants would be fun to play with.

He wonders why the farmer has put fences around the tomato plants.

Seward likes to hear the blue bird sing. If he is not still, he will scare the bird away.

The green grasshopper is hard to see on the ear of corn.

Everything seems to be busy on the farm.

Even the slippery earthworm
is getting breakfast.

Seward sees a turtle having a red strawberry for breakfast.

Seward hopes he can have watermelon for breakfast.

Here comes the farmer with some orange carrots.

Seward runs to catch up with the farmer.

Seward knows it is time for breakfast

Look for Seward's next Adventure

ABOUT the AUTHOR

When I was a little girl we got a Beagle puppy. He was named Seward's Folly. William Seward, Secretary of State for Pres. Lincoln, aided the USA in buying the Alaskan Territory. It was called Seward's Folly. Daddy named our dog for his relative. Seward was a great puppy going everywhere with us and sleeping in my bed! I am now a Grandmother and a Real Estate agent. I like to garden, sew, and give books to my family and friends. With my D.A.R. Chapter we also donate books to School Libraries around the country. I hope you enjoy reading about my dog and all the fun we had.

About the Illustrator

As a girl, I grew up learning how to draw from my dad and improved my art skills over the years with practice and schooling. I've always had a love for animals, so being able to take that passion for creatures and apply it to my art has been a goal throughout my artistic journey. Since earning my BFA in 2018, I have been growing my experience with commissions and freelance work. I have illustrated two other children's books about animals over the last year, and want to continue furthering my illustration career through design and storytelling. I am a full-time artist when I'm not at my day job, and with the support of my fiancé and two adorable cats, I hope to continue bringing characters to life and sharing my artwork with the world.

Made in the USA
Columbia, SC
25 February 2024